Carousel

A DISTILLATION OF TIME

Carousel
A DISTILLATION OF TIME

Phyllis Hotch
New & Selected Poems

NIGHTHAWK PRESS
TAOS, NEW MEXICO

Carousel: A Distillation of Time

Copyright © 2019 Phyllis Hotch

All rights reserved.

No part of this publication may be reproduced
or transmitted in any form or by any means, electronic
or mechanical, including photocopying, recording, or any
other information storage and retrieval system, without
the written permission of the publisher.

Published by Nighthawk Press.
Printed in the United States of America.

ISBN: 978-0-99868-078-1

Cover image: *WuLi Dancing,* © Ginger Mongiello
Author photo: Ramsey Scott

Also by Phyllis Hotch

A Little Book of Lies
No Longer Time
3 A.M.

Love and Gratitude
Janet, Ramsey, Larry

Table of Contents

Preface ... i
Chartres ... 1
The Work of Living Consumes ... 3
Now It's Piaf ... 4
You Are the Sun ... 5
Blues ... 6
Nocturne ... 7
Carousel ... 8
Distillation of Time ... 10
Unfolding ... 11
Synchrony ... 12
Yearning ... 13
Cracking the Code ... 14
Perseus ... 15
Hollow ... 16
Phenomena ... 17
A Suffusion of Blue Moths ... 19
Steel Song ... 20
Continuum ... 22
Shadows and Silhouettes ... 24
Burnings ... 25
Falling, Falling ... 27
Plum Island ... 28
Women I Know ... 29
Close ... 31
It's Evening ... 32
Dark ... 33
Winter Night in Provincetown ... 34
Come Flying ... 35
High Desert ... 37

Life Moves with Urgency ... 38
Frugal Repast ... 39
Clouds of Autumn ... 42
Blood ... 43
Dreaming Monkeyshines ... 44
Shadow ... 46
Anger ... 47
Chants of Childhood ... 48
Prayer ... 49
Ghazal ... 50
Fourth of July ... 51
Glass Suite ... 54
Hawk ... 58
Raven ... 59
Snapdragons ... 60
Goatsbeard ... 61
Orchid ... 62
Beauty Heals ... 63
Two White Peonies ... 64
August First at John Dunn Bridge ... 65
Disappearances ... 67
A Dry Winter ... 68
Gorge Bridge ... 70
Kossa ... 72
Spring Thaw ... 73
Bosch Revisited ... 74
She Glitters ... 75
Old Man ... 76
Bodies Within ... 77
Hat ... 78

Notes ... 82

Preface

Once again, poet Phyllis Hotch has given us a collection of poetry that is mesmerizing in its beauty and extraordinary in its poetical imagination. Each poem is written in a language that is both melodic and enchanting. Hotch is able to address the complexity of human emotions, the passing of time, and the questions about the meaning of a life well lived.

This is a poetry that encompasses nostalgia and longing, as well as the memory of the dead and the memory of the ones we have loved, without sentimentality but with the deep understanding of what love is and what love is missing in all of us. There are also poems about places and monuments, cathedrals, the vastness of the sea and the earth; and yet, each poem contains a unique and original world that the poet so bravely gives to its readers.

This is a poetry that does not hold back. It is authentic in its transparent emotions. In the poem "Phenomena," the first verse represents the spirit of the collection:

> All that is required lives within us:
> Breath and desire and laughter.

> Every love will be lost by
> death or change or distance.

With delicacy, Phyllis Hotch invites us to read her work many times, as each verse is filled with the profound questions we are often so afraid to ask. The poet writes about growing old, the fastness of time and seasons, and our bodies that age. She poses fundamental questions, such as How does one cope with the fear of not having lived with meaning? These questions appear as a constant thread in this collection. There are no clear answers but an invitation to live in plenitude.

The poem "Orchid" inspires us to think about the world that surrounds us:

> Petals like skin
> on sweet milk.
> Translucent,
> sensual and aware,
> …
> We want beauty
> To be more than beauty.

In these magnificent verses, Phyllis Hotch speaks to us about the marvelousness of the everyday and the necessity to seek a beauty that is healing and redeeming, a beauty that is all around us; but there is also a beauty that requires searching deeper inside ourselves.

There are poems about white peonies, about frogs that are disappearing, and, most solemnly, poems about aging. But these are not poems that convey the darkness of time passing. On the contrary — to age is to affirm life itself, to remember the memory of a body in love with the intensity and innocence of an adolescent, like in the poem "Close":

> I am older now than when they were old
> Much older than when they died
> …
> Voices
> I can hear the song — slightly
> off pitch…

This is a collection of great beauty and intensity. Hotch has mastered the craft of poetry, and this is her most superb work. The poet is also demanding of her readers. She is complex and direct, a voice that asks and demands we answer. Her poems will inspire us to think about how to live and how to die.

Bravo for this spellbinding collection that is evocative and haunting. Please read each poem as if entering a river of deep fluidity and boundless sound.

Marjorie Agosin

Chartres

On the east wall of the cathedral
little plants grow between ledges,
gutters and lintels. The old stones rise,
every story different, curves and recesses,
pillar, niches, black splotched, moss covered,
worn, not any less beautiful than when young.

Witnesses in the mist
wild doves hide and call
across the space from the wall
to the garden.
Murmurs like cries from hidden children,
souls from all the years these stones
have stood. White doves among the columns,
carvings, windows, arches. White
doves in the shadows.

Here, it is easy to accept the hope of heaven,
to understand why the bakers left their ovens
and carried stones, pushed barrows
and climbed, climbed to the tower, year
after year; the basket of bread
in the stained glass window is their testimony.

Now heaven is a wish.
Who would carry stones for a wish?
If I had a belief in the certainty of peace, angels

waiting for me, wouldn't I carry stones,
bring my bread, show my trust,
dream of paradise while sweat fills my eyes,
    and hands
cramp around the wooden spokes and I pull
to build, bear children, tell them to build?
Now, over the doorway, the birds sit on God's lap
and on the angular arm of the saint,
comfortable on the old stone.

Inside, Mary is ready. White
marble moving in a wind. Rising. Taking
all mothers' entreaties, all sons' fears
through the vault to heaven.
    In here carvings of gray stone,
blue and red glass show logical sequences,
justify promises to pilgrims in sandals who hope
    to meet
a spirit, hear stones speak, glass sing,
and watch glory rise from the floor.

The Work of Living Consumes

Mozart is laughing with us,
the earth turns, an old gramophone.
Hear this trill. It's a cuckoo.   Now stop.
The violin pleads with roses,
a cello's kindness,
soprano's silver.

Bring words to this morning, this euphoria,
to well-being, to living when others die,
when others suffer. Suffering
needs understanding to feel fingertips slide
counting vertebrae, soft fingertips to encircle
   the scapula.

Old men hold fears alone,
homeless hide in cartons.
Sofia leaves the ward
cradling an empty bunting — pink —
warm against her heavy breast.

How kind, the living believe
the dead to be resting
or that more is possible.

Now It's Piaf

From this little garden I can see Pedernal.
    An image of
O'Keefe's exotic lily joins my common garden:
cerise phlox, late-blooming hollyhocks in
    geometric ballet,
sweet voice in white pink cinnamon rose on
    yellow leaves,
sky blue innocence, bees scurry harvesting.
A mound of soft scented lavender recalls spring,
    but
I know this is October, however deceiving.

Last week the sun hid suddenly and wind
    proclaimed
King Cold's nearby. Swaying pines called time time
time, "and the days grow short when you reach
    September"
sings Ella's honey voice
floating over the drying roses,
spiced marigolds potted with purple verbena.
A sky covers white over blue.
No *should* in nature. Only time shrinking,
puzzling in all dimensions. Now it's Piaf's
tremolo   "…the autumn leaves drift past my
    window."

You Are the Sun

You are the sun on the chair
where the cat sleeps

You are the rock on the beach
when the surf rushes in

Not the empty train leaving the station
Not the deep gorge at sunset

I am a cascade in frozen January
I am overripe apricots under the tree, bees
    swarming

Not the wooden chair or the box lunch
    the man in work shoes carries
Not the beep of the microwave

You are the last turn of the pillow before sleep
    The drop of blood on the white blanket
Early morning wood smoke over the valley
    Chopin on Sunday afternoon
I am the orange streak at twilight
    The row of gray pots on the mantle

You will always be the sun on the chair

The rock in the surf
The white blanket
The grayblue smoke

Blues

Blues climb down and hang in rain-shine
those long-ago
hurting-hard blues

Blues
climb down
and hug your soul

Real down-blues
holler low
meet your hollow knees

Blues rest on
a soft bosom
Sweet and sad

Like Ella's slow song
with a plucked guitar
alongside

When your heart hides
the sorrow calls
short notes

Nocturne

Dusk reminds us days are short,
the shadows of pine and maple obscure
tangled roots in the evening.
Breeze carries the touch of a presence,
then breathing becomes panting.
Birds quiet in the thicket,
blue birds and rusty thrush,
invisible among the sumac leaves.
We stay close as the trail narrows
Ahead is a cabin with people
who will camp tonight.

We ask about the trail. Is it clear?
They offer space until daylight.
We have no blanket; we say goodbyes.
Coming dark holds fear
Moonlight helps
He trips but rises
I slide down the steepest slope

Last night's spectral visitor, who
woke me for the blood moon,
waves limpid hands above me.
We press between boulders.
Quicken the pace.
Reach level land in the dark.

Carousel

Time, you jump on my back
As if I were a circus pony
Made to ride the
Circle of my life

Time, you send loved ones
To waking dreams
As if clustered in robust
Raucous chorus
Around my bed

Then a young me
A flowered skirt
Gardenia corsage

Love lying side by side
While the ocean seeps closer
Ebbs in moonlight
We wait until morning
Return to sultry
City heat
Or the baby
In my arms
All mine at that moment

Only diurnal rhythms
Nothing delays you
Nothing quickens

Time, you bully liar
Mirrors torment
Indifferent
Even my visiting ghosts
Have lost shape

Distillation of Time

What is distillation but a heating and cooling
Stretching and shrinking
Like time in childhood
Long days increased by evenings
Playing in the glamorous dark hours
Maybe allowed to bring a glass jar
With a wide top
A stretched sheet of something sheer
Like wax paper pulled and punctured
To keep fireflies alive overnight
The nights perfumed with summer
Air filled with voices calling talking and peepers
*
Time hovered mechanically at the small cemetery
Already hot in the morning of a burning summer
Filling with new arrivals then with words
Readings carefully weighty reliably sincere
People standing sitting hushed
Looking at the burnt grass
Looking at the widow looking at the azure sky
Minutes stretched with no tears
Unheard liminal voices circling
Not yet not you not yet

Unfolding

Late afternoon in the high desert
can bring thunder and rain clouds.
Today the wind blows across the valley.
Gazinnias in the little garden fold their colors.
Vultures with their curved wings soar and swoop
playing on the light winds and
tormenting the small sparrows and finches
sequestered among the branches of the Russian
    olives.
Nighthawks who shot across and back
have gone off to roost in the dark.

Night is quiet in the high desert.
Hours pass in mute ballet.
The dead spread their web that captures,
saddening and comforting.
Voices never heard, formless spirits
denizens of the dark
more quiet than the quiet night,
more present than the stars.

Synchrony

Wind shakes and gathers
a dark sky
Groaning roofs
Racing time
    shrieks

Dark noon displaces even prayer
    Air the element rules
    Holds breath
disorder swirls
the questioner who fights catastrophe
      swept away

Past hour, past minute,
forgotten
Coming rain erases memory with moment

Yearning

Still dark when I came there.
His face was smooth, lips pale, hands slightly
    warm.
We waited
Together until it grew light and
They took him away, out the back door.

      In the morning when the sun is still in
        the east
      I wish his soul to be bright and free.
      Evening when the clouds
      Bloom apricot-rose in the west
      Day slips away
      At night stars are company,
      more real but unknowable.

Yearning for
A phantom remaining just beyond

the memory of a scent,
a mirage

Cracking the Code

After you left doors wouldn't close
Wind raped the trees

After you left stars sent cryptic messages with
bright promises in quaking tambourines

After you left I was certain you would come
to light white sage and smudge the dark

After you left I sent dragonflies dressed as drones
around the universe. I met Isis looking for bones

We swept the desert with feathers
I didn't catch a hair or tooth
Osiris sits in the dark. Where are you?

After you left I listened for whispers in
the rhythm of traffic lights and the geometry of
    jet streams
in the boxes piled high near Walmart. I thought
the messages might have been misaddressed
to tar patches on the roof.

But it's probable
time has collected all the messages

and saves them in starlight
for us to read.

Perseus

I.
Perseus cried how could I live without you.
He placed his head on earth's nurturing breast
    to sleep.

Old, very old. We lay close to feel warmth.
Skin. He lay his head beneath my chin.
Hand on my willing breast we slept. Short
or long minutes. Turned to sleep again.

When we were young, very young, we lay
close, breast to breast and thigh to thigh,
close. Worked to sweat, worked to love,
again. Slept again.

Turned away at last to sleep again.

II.
When we were old, we lay like white roses
    glowing in the cool of night.
When we were almost very old, we lay like orange
    marigolds in dry flame.
When we were old, but not quite ready to be old,
we lay like purple wilted hibiscus in the snow.

Hollow

Hollow
Aches heavy under flesh
Lives like lichen on
Huge mountain rocks
Grows like seaweed in ocean's coral reefs
Waits in an empty rain-barrel
Like hope
Spreads through the blood and
Back to the heart
Needy for a medium
Like transcendence — like repentance
Like prayers' tears
Or music rich from the breathing organ
Soft then full
Vibration alive open
Like in the gold of October

Phenomena

All that is required lives within us:
Breath and desire and laughter.
Every love will be lost by
death or change or distance.

Memory will arise like a dream,
a wind to carry music or scent of food
pungent and rich in the pot or forgotten
        and burnt.
Some memories circle
like birds around the feeder:
whitecapped sparrows, yellow finches.
Some sing.

Sunlight comes after snow and grayness.
Disappears again.

Sleep with a wish
and it becomes a dream.
        In the dream I complain with friends:
        "The bills are calling from every
            corner —
        how can I meet these demands?"

        Sympathetic smiles, nods.
        I continue fretting.
        He is two decades younger

than when he died.
He says, "Sell the Chevy, we don't need
   it now."
"Yes!" I say — I also am young.
"But when that's gone
what will we sell?"

I wake
and keep the dream for company.

Write the dream on a piece of paper
fold it in the pocket of jeans that
no longer fit.
Ride them on a small carousel
in a wild carnival.

That is when a dream becomes
a silent hope that speaks.

A Suffusion of Blue Moths

Loss sings in the blue fuzz
of a plaintive banjo,
in the clear tears of a muted trumpet
on nights when clouds
withhold the companionship of stars.

Steel Song
For Larry
Homage to Ted Egri, sculptor

Dynamite explodes in the bright desert
Roars, thrusts the corten steel
to soar, to rise against the blue,
become hawk's wings on the blue sky.
      Settled on the packed earth but
not yet born
too dense to fly
this belly needs to open
these arms need to point.
This soul needs to rise.
For what purpose?

What can propel such density?
The small man imagines a mountain
aims to free the black steel to
lift like a dove
light as a flute
rich as rolling drums
so he blasts again and again
until the bird rises to
mime the mountain
until circles hold angled wings
and the wind sees its shape
Sings

Men bring their sticks and sit to drum
The hollow steel throbs
calls to the past
drums to an unknown future.
They feel the spirit of the mountain
and the man is satisfied.

Continuum

1
The old live aware of time running
but they can't run. Sam Oeur told me
how he and his family fled Phnom Penh,
whipped forward by Pol Pot's demons.
His young son and pregnant wife and
old mother who could not keep up, but
not to keep up meant to be killed and
rot at the roadside. So she
kept up and lived.

2
New Orleans flooded,
stranded residents in the nursing homes.
Weak.   Waiting in the smelly dark.

3
Old women and men laugh about their bodies,
don't talk about it. Prefer stories, their
love affairs. They observe:
passing crowds, strange undress, alien language,
baffling technology, foreign food.
They accept: their days
depend on human love finding them.

4
Very old ones sit. They observe, ponder, how did I raise kids, jobs, cars:
red, black, silver.   Now sit,
remember a name of no consequence.

5
They think of the
mysterious eminence who will
escort them to bliss or some vastness for which
they are never quite ready.
They listen for words from soft lips,
Laughter thick and sweet like summer fruit.
Remember a loved one's name. Tears.
Old people's tears run so easily.

Shadows and Silhouettes

When daylight fills with music and
darkness previews regret
thoughts move to a wilderness,
travel alone
in past and present
to seek the aloneness
a discoverer who welcomes unknown wilderness
moves into dark woods undaunted by
lion leopard or wolf.

Wilderness holds a sorceress, creator of mirage,
enchantress of deep dreams
who can be deadly. Be prepared
to wander in the past,
find faces and weightless bodies
not quite erased. Follow a voice without sound to
a storytree whose branches snag. Winds.
Keep moving — lightning, hail, and
heat of protestation.

Leave no trace.

Burnings

1
The calm mountain holds vigil.
A long line of trees
climbs along the river
to a sacred lake.
Peaks roll south
show geometrics
of past fires on their slopes.
Green fields stretch below
a bright blue sky.
A rare red fox runs through
and many prairie dogs and skunks.

2
Turkey vultures soar.
Occasional eagles.
Flying birds:
bluebirds, blue jays, blue-gray piñon jays
hide from the sweeping vultures,
soft gray doves, their hoarse calls over and over
hummingbirds sweeping past
little cliff swallows guard six speckled eggs
in a nest above the doorway.

3
North of the mountain is El Salto,
by fable, a lover's leap.
Going south the lower slopes show history
with patches of recent aspen where juniper
and piñon grew before the fires.
Without good rain the old trees dry.
Brush and grass dries,
A fool's mistake destroyed a community.

4
Now fire rages near and far:
immolation arson lightning overturned autos.
San Tropez, Corsica, California, London.
In Somalia fire punishes the oppressed.
Fire followed by smoke ashes and rampaging
    famine,
The blaze from gods roars and smolders,
Eats the past.
Falling, Falling

I wrote on the card, "falling,
falling" from Rilke's poem, seeing
myself, or a simulacrum, scrambling through air
    woozy with
effort to allay the thud of impact.

The subject is death, falling to
my epitaph, a quarrel with time. Falling

outraged, using life infused at birth to rage with
    talon and fang
red and wild as any creature seeking a witness
    who does not appear.
Death matters.

Not only birth matters. Death lives too.
Six million, thirty-two million, maybe one more
    million from Darfur
soon. A bumper crop

to compost: falling autumn leaves, notes on a
    scale,
meteors in August, motes lighting the heavens.

Plum Island

Contemplate pastoral scene hushed, verdant
trees arched over a curved path
light filtered on silvered leaves
then the table shakes
and the puzzle breaks along fine lines into
small odd meaningless shapes
Like life

Watch a wave
grow taller whiter
capture someone sunning on the beach
Swept away
Detritus
in a green sea

Women I Know

Women seventy eighty ninety are not afraid
    at night.
One goes to bed at eight p.m. One sleeps from
    five a.m. to ten.
They know waking will be painful, back stiff,
    feet slow.
Daylight comes as a surprising gift. Some will read.
Some will write, cook or dress, feed the cats.
    One will
call the one who waits. Some will help the
    neighbor.
Some will be hungry, count the pennies, pills
    and beans.
Hope her luck kicks in again. One will count her
wrinkles and one feed the wood stove.
One has bright orange hair. One hides
the empty spot beneath a hat.
Some hands tremble
Some still type and text and play piano.
One will walk, one drive, another sit.
Some don't see as well, hear as well,
chew as well or stand straight.
One will use a walker.
One will grab her skis. One will fall.
One primps for coffee with her group. One drinks
Nescafé with powdered cream. She dreams
of oceans she has never seen. One flies New York

to Hong Kong again. One had
six surgeries, one moved four thousand miles.
A son comes by each morning, one's daughter
 never.

Close

I'm older now than when they were old
Much older than when they died

I do something ordinary on a too-quiet morning
and think — *Tomorrow I'll see him*
or her
and I look up because
they seem close
nearer than they ever used to be

Voices
I can hear the song — slightly
off pitch
when she sang
I can see the smile deep in the corners of her
    mouth
and hands
a notch in the cuticle

Way back
I didn't ask them to help me
Now I do

It's Evening

Gray evening, chilly.
I'm wearing your big and
Soft burgundy sweater
With the moth hole in front.
One year since you died,
I knew you were
Dying, two weeks before when
You did not want to talk or eat.

There really was not much to say.

Afterward I mostly missed your touch.
And what we could not have,
Because we never knew
many parts of ourselves.
We knew what held us together,
primitive flesh and blood. Simple, warm.
But not what pulled us apart.

Old age comes on as a surprise,
We were busy—
and then we were old.
Trial by fire.

Dark

Whispering everywhere
scraps of stories
unstrung notes
      day promises
      darkness presses
Night is a pliant envelope of
nevers and unknowns

Winter Night in Provincetown

A small house only steps from ocean rush
arrogant, demanding.
Over and over.

Everything winter cold: salt scented air
screaming power of water
dominating dark, absolute sea.

We were flesh holding sorrow between us,
our bodies warming
with rare communion,

perishable, transient.
Incessant wavesound.
Our feeble heat gift enough.

Come Flying
After Elizabeth Bishop

Come flying loved ones missed and needed
Come whooshing through soundwaves and
    gunshots
radar scanners drones cameras, radio, tweeters
    and cyber spies.

Gus, father, straight and strong as when I could fly
come over the glitz of Taj Mahal and the Palisades'
    Ferris wheel
Mother Mae in her blue cornflower hat,
Brother Gil, 10 years old, carving initials in the
    furniture
come shake your fists at the TV news
tell them what a predictable mess they've made
fly under the jet trails, over the helicopters at
    Holy Cross

Come flying, glamorous music teacher, Lotte from
Germany with tear-filled eyes
we will walk, arms linked like ladies. You will
    translate Goethe
Come small Nettie knowing South Carolina
Come listen to the chants
Come Julius and Naomi, geniuses without money
    in a loft

Sy, come flying in the bathtub, listening to
    Brahms, tell me
how to calculate the algebra of cunning and
    deceit
Come flying little Zaide, you bested the tsar
    to cross
an ocean. Tell me how to survive this century
Come flying at night, in starlight, down
the handle of the big dipper, right through my
    window

High Desert

Step among brittle sage
and sharp tumbleweeds.
Avoid snakeskins and coyote bones.

Pass luminal walls that
rise and disappear,
walls of the insane house,

where the never forgotten
and the lost sit among
brown and gray sage.

My shadow
staring at the sky,
holds a shoe for the one who left.

Life Moves with Urgency

The digits are clear but the meaning opaque.
Impossible to understand old age.
Each day unfolds with quotidian tasks
Faced simply: brush, dress, eat,
swallow a handful of pills,
walk — grateful for a smooth path.

The black hills of my mind beckon to paths
paved with words,
stories fill an amethyst sky,
and the crickets question
what color will suffuse the last moment.

Frugal Repast
(Picasso, Paris, Autumn, 1904)

Neither one of us sees
the dark wine bottle and the piece of bread
on the rumpled tablecloth.

We cannot eat,
our hunger is too great.
He sits close to me but looks sharply to the far
    corner.

Our bodies are not touching.
One long hand is awkward around my elbow,
one near my shoulder. I won't move.

He sits close to stifle the echoes
of yesterday's curses.
Tonight, he cannot speak.

What can we say?
A piece of bread is not enough.
Where is there more?

Under these hard lights
he is the shadow of my immobility.

"I will rise and go now."
— W. B. Yeats

Clouds of Autumn

Cumulus clouds
on virginal blue:

white fantasies of floating
fill the sky

Our tired souls
seek rest with them

above our
bloodied earth

Blood

The message on TV forewarns viewers.
The father howling carries his bloodied child:
the plane did not hear him, nor the drone, nor
    the missile
nor the gun, nor the bomb.
Nor the child,
now inert and red in his arms. No one is listening:
not the gun bearing live bodies on mission,
not the white-haired (or dark) legislators
who cannot produce black-and-white pages
to accomplish truce or peace, only
realignment called strategy.

Tomorrow the blood will be black.
Snow will fall and then drops will be red.

Dark will hide it until sunrise
glowing glorious opal.

Dreaming Monkeyshines

Monkeys falling.
Saturation bombing covers the sky like Dresden.
That happened for spite, passion enough to erase
a manifestation of beauty, but pride too.
These monkeys, three-inch plastic, with curved
    legs and tails
toss them, loop them over a rod, catch them on a
    finger if you can.
Red ones, some in green and yellow and pink
ISIS no doubt. Remember when Castro opened
    the jails

sent us the good and the bad, beaten and tossed
    in open boats
could drown or be shot on the beaches, now the
    monkeys
are falling from Malawi, from South Africa, from
    Syria, Ethiopia,
Yemen, Ukraine. Close the sky, kill the children.

How can we know which monkey is a good
    monkey?
The sky is full of monkeys, like Canadian geese,
like mad squawking apes, like gorillas with bombs
tucked in their mouths, under their tails, in the sky.

Close the sky, dig a trench, get the FBI CIA Special
    Forces cops
Get everyone, give them guns, give them
    automatics.
Be ready, call it a red day for monkeys.
Where are they coming from?

Shadow

An aperture has a shadow

Shadow devours the tree and the soil,
claims the notes of a hymn,
summons a lost land with foreboding.

Shadow without substance everywhere,
sequestered niche or congested highway,
follows the feet of a wedding march,
weightless, carries the weight of the world.

Snow leopard blending on the rocky slope,
tensed to leap fifty feet for the twitching hare,
jaguar hunts the zebra, shadow haunts them all.
Coyote lopes along the road. Knows it well.

A little boy wears a turned-around cap,
skims the cement on his roller skates. Unaware.

The mountain stands calm framed in the window,
feels the sadness of the ocean rising,
but the earth beneath footsteps shifts like sand.
Anger sends the scent of blood.
There is no understanding,
Without understanding there is shadow.

Anger

lives in the body
        demands blood bones and offal
avenging angels victorious villains
        stretches time minute between minute
between think and forget

carries a knapsack of smoldering stones, a bellyful
    of regret
        hears a silent roar
curses again
        shoots again

Chants of Childhood
For the Kosovar on the evening news
who is coming to America

He studies what to remember.
Every movement necessary history:
how she cooked the eggs for breakfast,
where they ate
who sold the cucumbers on market day
what money looked like on payday
children holding hands at school.
He will begin a new life
one like ours.

He will come burdened with emptiness
and will leap into the glut
of wheels chips discs digits
that will crowd out the chants of childhood
with food, wet kisses.
                    Soon
he will look more like us. Individuals:
one plus one plus lonely one
each building a self by the hour
choice by choice and thing by thing.

Prayer

My mother prayed silently over Sabbath candles.
She did it alone.
At my bedtime she recited *now I lay me down,*
I did not know what *if I should die* really meant.
I did not know where I kept my soul.
It did not comfort me.

When my brother left for the South Pacific in
    the war
we prayed together in the little storefront that
served as a chapel in the neighborhood.
Seats filled every Friday evening.
At night, every night, I read the psalms.
That helped sleep.
My brother came home changed,
Thinner and quiet.

One can pray, I have been told,
one hundred times a day in gratitude.
Turn east, the sun rises in the east
to a new day.
The moon rises in the east
in the limitless cosmos
and we may lie down in peace for a while.

Ghazal

Our mountain is gray today my love
I hold its grayness quiet in my hands

No songs. Not robin nor meadowlark sang today
but piñon jays looked for seed in my hands

Sleepless restless I may wander today
with tenderest lightning, hope in my hands

Find me. Which way today to find you
to show you my heart full of blood in my hands

See, our children, they say today
with apricot blossoms filling their hands

White lavender smoke today my love
close to your lips, your hair in my hands

Stay with me. Sleep with me. Stay today.
The sound of your breath, your smell in my hands

Joy today. My name today is joy,
I remember your laughter in my hands.

Fourth of July

The Girls' Marching Band stretches from curb
    to curb
        a banner held beneath the almost covered
        belly buttons
LET FREEDOM RING
    Red white and blue

    They step forward, sweating
under July sun, ahead of the red convertibles
    carrying
        mayor, councilmen, former sheriffs,
        veterans of wars long ago and recent
        neat olive drab and shiny buttons.

    On the curb three reservists in camouflage
    and thick boots
(impassive uncomfortable) arms
    behind them turn away from a shriek.
Lacy-ruffled tiny girl has dropped her blue
    popsicle.

    The beautiful young, becoming-believing
the right-to-happiness-life cluster near the U.S.
    Army table
        holding in two fists five senses
circling the new day night day. All
    even the brightest don't know this hustle.

Bland boy-faced man with unblinking eyes near
        their own younger faces giddy with choice
           (desire glamour).
They don't watch his tail, his stinger.
      Recruiter
for freedom. Better for him than the dusty white
    heat of the war. Closer

       the boy to his child bride. She wears his
          gold ring and little shining stone
she twists and twists on her finger. No glance
    toward tomorrow. Today this means
        independence. Behind the transports the
          bugles and drums. Rat tat Souza
trombones in out in out under the sun,
    neat olive drab and shiny buttons.

After the four cowboys thick-bodied in snug
    shirts, straw hats over red faces
        girl on the gleaming horse, silky against
           its curving flanks
her dark ponytail proud as her mare's.

Women on the sidewalk shake the
　　　sleeping infants in their strollers.
　　　The tall shapely one
though no longer so young holds her two-year-old tightly.
　　　　He's her identity (protective and wise).
His plump arm on her neck. The checks come
　　　every month. The dad stays away.
　　　　Her fridge empty again. Stern with the boy,
　　　　she's the boss.
Red white and blue flag in his hand.

　　　　More floats — women in white sunbonnets,
　　　　men in top hats
and star-spangled blue jeans, old folks sitting in
　　　aluminum folding chairs
　　　　catch candy tossed by teenagers from cars
　　　　trailing streamers.

Balloons go up. Music spirals up.

Glass Suite

Arcs everywhere:
The comet at sunset
Can you find it, she asked?

Curving into evening
elusive and magical
pursuing its journey.

We turn
to look again.

*
Eight around the table after dinner,
Candle light and cut glass,
colors cast across the table
refraction splitting white light.
> One voice raucous, one voice subdued.
> Smiles that are not smiles.
> Lowered chin,
> Mississippi, San Bruno,
> again the bus ride.
> Shouted words loud as the hoses.

Red orange green blue light
fragmenting into the dim
late hour. Smiles.

>   Why smiles
>   for past events
>   sinister or humiliating?

Glass fragments aglow
reflect on their faces.

*

Mirror boxes hold treasures old
stamps single earrings pennies.
Delighting tinkling. A tiny glass bell.
"Mirror, mirror on the wall…" Deceitful.

*

Mirrors on the black giants a hundred stories high.
Rain slid across the black glass
then dust flew
streaked and splashed
made it gray in the morning sun.

Sand turned molten becomes transparent
heavy or tissue thin.
Storefronts become mirrors.
That's no stranger walking by.

*

A glass storefront falls in the dark,
A sleek locus to register rage, release
lethal confetti.

Men ram the rear window of the police car.
Crystal curse
shatters over and over on every newscast.
Then the men shake the car.

Splinters under shoes
in Missouri, Staten Island, Cleveland,
splinters of glass.
Bottles in alleys: pints, half pints, slim singles.
Shards of glass
hold the scrabble on the hill.

Splinters of glass shards pave the empty lot
 between streets.
Brown, green, midnight blue, clear
glisten in noon sun.

*
Beach glass nestled into sand
scratched and slapped by the waves,
scraped against rocks,
from wines bottle or milk bottles.
Not a lethal dagger. Vital,
becoming precious like an old face shrunk
translucent eyes milky with cataract.

*

Glass. She said she would make
shaped birds. Arcs
sweeping toward the horizon.

*

The dove has left her imprint on the window.
Faint elegant graceful ghost.

Hawk

White circle insignia on the underside
curved wings' arabesque

Beady eyes inspect terrain
rushing below:
brush, shrubs, sage, elms, red ditches, rocks

Spirals higher wider
expands the search
Targets a plump
Prairie-dog cottontail
a cat who might move,
a sparrow
will wait still as stone among
leaves of the Russian olive
not thrilled by grace and swirl overhead
of a machine who also eats

Raven

Not a demon
as he might look
perched on a post
dark against the evening sky
or soaring with wings spread.

A clown here
at the Sonic on a pleasant evening
stopping for a quick snack.
He stands. I wait for a stentorian speech
from this guy who looks like a corpulent mayor.

No raucous trills, quarks or knocks
because there are no morsels.
Legs wide apart appraising
surveys the clean concrete.
Lustrous black among the cartoon colors
of the menus, pauses at each parked car,
continues waddling,
taking his time
bucks against the wire trash basket.
Was it truly accidental?
Did he plan to leave this mess behind?

Snapdragons

Upright and dependable
they stand against the hard west wind
Pink white bright yellow
like palace guards in thick bearskin helmets

with a name that fits and easy to remember.
Blossoms that entertain little soft fingers.
Squeeze. Make the furry tongues flap.
Make us smile.

Goatsbeard

A wildflower, with flashy yellow blooms or purple
    plumes,
worldwide traveler who flies,
but loves field and edge.

Hated everywhere, *Tragopogon*, in Latin, *salsifis*
    in French.
Wildflower with furry stems. Noxious weed,
detested even in deserts where chamisa and

dandelions get a nod. Avoid this one.
Bristles that can kill a horse, wound a dog.

Orchid

Petals like skin
on sweet milk.
Translucent,
sensual and aware,

more aware than they are:
as rocks appear powerful and
knowing their history.

Large people seem
brave and noble.
Beautiful people
seem kind and loving.

We want beauty
to be more than beauty.

Beauty Heals

Ignore
cacophony of stress
tigers of night dreams
satanic predictions
whispered,
grimaces behind doors.

Think of words like
silver not sliver
hallelujah not heil
caress not carcass
smile not smolder.

Beauty warms tight tendons
creased foreheads.
Beauty heals. Love
emanates from eyes.
Love blooms with lilac blossoms

Look up.
White gold behind dark clouds
oboes velvet call.

Two White Peonies

Admire without touching
the sweet velvet of petals.
Breathe vague fragrance
of an old rose.

There is the there.
Like a child in death
still lovely
and accepting love's promises of
heaven's flowers, all colors shapes.
Blossoms on woody stems
bowing toward bottom
stand as mute companions.

Like the calla lily huge and filled with gold
like the iris sculpted for drama or
lilac wafting lavender.
This peony wilted with dark tipped petals
bends, as if blessing a stone-lined grave.

August First at the John Dunn Bridge

We sat at the edge of the river on the pebbly slant.
Sweet water scent, light voices of young girls, and
boys teasing them to jump.

Behind us and before us the gorge rocks,
huge sharp-cornered squares and rectangles
    rising
on each other's shoulders.

We rest or play in their domain,
grateful visitors wanting only their tolerance.
Water moves clear and calm. Breezes.

The Rio Grande is very narrow here
Across the river a group wades,
two young men and two young women with
    babies.
The baby in the blue plastic raft cries.

Its cries come clearly across the silky slow water,
but south of the small steel bridge
water pushes, rushing against rocks making
    music.

We sit until nearly sunset holding this peaceful
    present
boxed in the unknown past,

memorize the glistening river,
drive to the top of the canyon walls.

Daylight diminishes. We
move into the sky
blue green mauve gray, a slender line of red.
Utterly silent black rocks.

Disappearances

Frogs are disappearing worldwide and we don't
    know why
and the cacao plants too will
disappear if the midge that inhabits the seed
can't survive because the canopy of trees has
    been
cut down and the red fox with silky fur and sharp
    teeth

but what has happened to the frogs' furious
    cacophony
filling the woodlands and swamplands
infusing night with prophecy of summer
music of sheer energy
pulsing dissonance of untuned guitars

A Dry Winter

Solemn mountain
Dry in a dry sky
In a gray evening
A coyote stands on the edge of the cliff

Three sparrows sift among the gravel
Drink from the stone basin
The coyote's jaw opens and closes

Windchimes play crazily
Cold wind crawls along Coyote's
lean limbs
tail tucked

Voices lifted down the road carry

Overhead crows croak
Sail on the wind
A call from across the mesa
Once twice
A chorus for nightfall

Icicles hung from the gutters last winter
Ice coated the path
A shadow slides across the window
Snow patches glowed in moonlight

Coyote calls in the moonlight

Alone for this search
Rabbit dog cat
Coyote waits
Magpies wait for him

Loping gait sureness arrogance
Stops on a wall   Walks
Each step correctly balletic

Euphony
A chorus in the dark
Anguished yelps and howls

Fear of trucks
Did he just pass the southside?
Did he see the cats near the gate?

The river is moving
barely wet between the banks

No snow
Blackbirds sit in the juniper tree
Coyote waits in the open sagebrush
Ignores the fox who flashes past

Gorge Bridge

Hoofbeats on the steel bridge
beat louder than the cars and trucks. Two ponies.
A broad shouldered Indian rides the creamy white.
On his black hair a gold scarf. Behind him
a black pony with silver mane and tail,
sleek and small, follows on a lead.
They beat the steel bridge, command attention,
cross the road, and descend the steep rock.
Loose white sleeves last to be seen.

People drive to the bridge then walk across,
    unprepared.
One man in his Western hat laughs, amazed.
A little girl holds her gray-haired grandma's hand,
steps stiff and timid, arm extended,
her pink satin purse suspended, swings.
A good-looking man with a dark mustache
escorts his family. A tiny child howls in fear
as space runs past the fence railings.
He frowns at his cowardly daughter.

In brilliant sunshine the bridge seems white,
belongs to the blue air. Land moves sensuously
on each side. Mountains and mesa
change with sunlight and clouds.
Stretching east the road makes ripples over
    each rise.
Westward a long expanse flows to mountains,

and the dark gorge in morning shadow plunges
from upward thrust of ridges and mountains
to the silent river far below,
to hidden beginnings.
Water did not erode this rock. It shifted
with heaves and groans, it split.
Now the river travels through.
The gorge cuts towards center,
more than one lifetime deep.

Kossa
*Kossa (Pueblo Clown), Paul Joseph Speckled Rock,
Lithograph 1981*

Bright clowns dance along white museum walls.
In square frames small figures painted orange
    and black
shake their sticks. In beaded moccasins
they crouch and stomp toward the far corner
where Kossa hangs:

He stands in a gray winter
twilight on black sand patched with snow.
Turquoise splashes the ends of his scarf
deerskin tassels hang from his armbands.
Black and white stripes ring his legs and body and
the antlers he wears on his head.
Dressed to clown he stares through black
    encircled eyes
past the dim sky
and does not laugh.

Spring Thaw

No bells from the church
No birdsong

Under a darkening sky
She pauses to consider

Her shawl has
tulip red and yellow stripes

but only brown resistant mud
sucks at her moccasins

so she stands at the bright
edge of snow

feels the familiar tug and push
of tasks and wishes

and walks again, hoping
lilacs in each slippery step

Bosch Revisited

This is a large painting, horizontal rectangular. Not
a violated bull but a
naked pale pink girl in a white lace bra
on a black rug. Her legs thrust apart
between them a young man,
his face away. Her face
twisted, mouth wide in red terror.
The background: shining towers of a city,
on the right a college campus green cultivated.
A cross on the chapel. Cerulean sky. Cumulus
    clouds. Pastel drones.
A fat guy in a bill cap, well-tailored suits,
scattering of pills, needles, discarded utensils.
Guns and automatics and rifles to the left.
Little scenes placed around the canvas:
figures of women being raped in cars.
Old and new cars, fancy ones, beat up.

We see her face: But
his face? What does he look like? Is his mouth
turned down in contempt or turned up in
    satisfaction?

A bright yellow ribbon unfurls across the bottom,
six-packs, beer cans, whiskey,
wine bottles delicately drawn,
shaped like a smile (or a grimace).

She Glitters

She glitters brightly golden
Her dress
Gold sequins closely placed
Her shoes too
Gold with slender straps across
Her arched insteps
There is no denying she's seductive
And like Richard Cory
She glitters when she walks
We follow at a short distance
Avoid detection. Is this stalking?
She does not know.

We do not plan to approach her.
Her hips roll rhythmically
Show practice. There is no denying
She is attractive though vulgar
What lures to the glitter
That cannot serve?

Old Man

A weary old man
At the side of the road
Alone
Waited alone
Holding bony knees
Trousers worn soiled
On bony shanks
Shoes worn torn
On the long road
Long hair long beard
Thirsty tongue in a dry mouth
"Is this the place to wait?"
Asked the clouds
"Where will it take me?"
Took hold of the sky
Stood to continue
Followed the road

Bodies Within

Framed in the doorway under the arch.
Squared, your arms distanced from your sides,
enraptured you look across the valley
breathing the light
looking past three brown horses grazing.

Beneath the dark shirt
familiar flesh. I touch the place
beneath the arm under the brown soft hair
know the acid aroused sweat smell
heat under your chin   heat of your groin.

> I see the body before this one — straighter —
> that would stamp heavily upstairs
> to stand and look past the porch
> to green pines, would run down the back
> stairs to the yard
> to the silky spring grass
>
> almost like the body within that one —
> slipping across mine
> hands cool trembling
> aching, water around us rocking us, cooling
> cradling as we caressed, too intent to smile
> then smiling

Do you see me too? All the layers at once?

    Do you see the light hair, long legs wrapped
        around you
    wide eyes believing truth spoken through
        teeth and tongue
    in the rightness of curve of throat, curve
        of belly,
    arch of foot? Do you see through the body
    as through a rounded light to small breasts
        that urge
    to slim knees bending and straightening,
    soft fingers opening
    and closing
    into bodies we thought we'd left?

Years ago my daughter asked
when she was not quite ready to lose the self
    she'd known —
Do we leave behind what we were?
No, I said with sudden certainty   *no*   we take it
    with us
grow like the rings of a tree, the same tree
    adding on
more deeply textured. Do you see

the woman through the skin
like a body outlined
against the fabric of a tent lit from within,
like a body backlit from a fire set on hard-packed
    earth
transparent in the darkness?

We traveled. We travel
over peaks and brown desert through water
    and air
to enter transparent
selves within — seeing the man you were
within the man you are — seeing the woman I am
over the woman I was
lit by the red sun behind us.

Hat

"O…come back to teach me again…"
　—Edward Hirsch

Black hat on the walnut
　　　　　　　　chest
Greet the hat with silence
　　Look away
　　　　　Like Asian custom
　　　　Politeness　respect
Small slouch-hat, black-ribbed fabric
Surface captures
　　　　Dust
　on the narrow brim
Endowed with a sly smile and
power of play
worthy of marigolds or
smudge-smoke
Thought intrudes: move it to the closet.
　　　　Restraint born of need
　　　　stronger than pride
　　　　humility reigns
　　facing eternity.

Acknowledgments

With gratitude for your generous support and friendship...

Marjorie Agosin
Marianne Furedi
Lise Goett
Veronica Golos
Ariana Kramer
Ginger Mongiello
Barbara Scott
Carol Terry

Notes

Chartres	*Wildwood Press*
Frugal Repast	*The Threepenny Review*
Kossa	Ritual figure, Pueblo painting, Millicent Rogers Museum
Spring Thaw	Ekphrastic Exhibit Painting by Bill Baron
Bosch Revisited	Hieronymus Bosch
Bodies Within	*3 A.M.*, Three A Taos Press

About the Author

It is my good fortune to live in a place that loves art, a community rich with beauty and artists, with bountiful people who generously support and enrich each other with their talents. I know this has contributed to my many years of writing poetry and to my long life.

During my years in Massachusetts, I taught English, humanities, and creative writing, then began writing seriously. I organized workshops and events as arts coordinator for Arts Wayland, which led to publishing chapbooks for the winners of contests judged by noted poets. Later, in Taos and active in SOMOS, there were many events featuring nationally and internationally known guest artists and poets to speak out for free expression and justice. My husband always provided support, though his love was math and physics.

Publication of each book has been a gift, from the first one, *A Little Book of Lies,* which is humor enhanced with art by African American activist Doris Fields. Next came *No Longer Time,* a heartfelt expression of loss for my eldest daughter, who died of breast cancer; the third book is *3 A.M.,* facing life after heart attacks and my husband's Alzheimer's.

During these tumultuous times, as we await the marvels to come and hold fast to what is beautiful and important, I work on both poetry and prose, on observations and reflections. Age creates the lens to view the challenges and surprises.

www.ingramcontent.com/pod-product-compliance
Lightning Source LLC
Chambersburg PA
CBHW031203090426
42736CB00009B/769